Single to First Date

Short Attention Span Guide to Dating

Single to First Date

How to Meet the Right Woman and Get the First Date

John J. Gillies,

Artwork by Jill Krynicki

Foreword by Dr. Laurie J. Moroco, Ph.D.

Sawle Register Service
Madison

The information this book reflects the opinion of the author.

First published 2009 in the United States by Sawle Register Service.

All illustrations by Jill Krynicki

ISBN: 0-9824750-2-0

ISBN-13: 978-0-9824750-2-7

To Amy. I miss you every day.

Foreword

A "search for intimacy"[1] began in the late 1970's and continues to gain momentum decades later. According to Montgomery, "It is not surprising, therefore, that the ideal of intimacy has become a major theme in the scholarly study of interpersonal communication"[2]. It has been called bonding, intimacy, unity, and interpersonal connection - a "critical component of the human experience"[3] and a moral good[4].

Communication - both verbal and nonverbal - is the primary vehicle for achieving closeness. People who are unable to share in most thoughts and feelings with others may experience a painful form of loneliness that Weiss[5] calls emotional isolation. Men and women alike are searching for relationships in order to fulfill a human need called intimacy. Literally, intimacy means to "get into another person" in order to know that person as a unique human being[6]. Intimacy is important for many reasons, according to Hook, Gerstein, Detterich, and Gridley[7], which include human development, intrinsic appeal, and overall well-being. And furthermore, without a positive and intimate connection with other human beings, a person may suffer from physical, interpersonal, and emotional difficulties that can be harmful[8].

Easier said than done. Fortunately, this book is a refreshing and tidy text that deviates from the norm of self-help books by offering a practical workbook that combines theory and practice for successful relationship development and maintenance. Written by a man for men, the book does a superb job of illuminating themes necessary for healthy relational development, particularly open communication, honesty, and respect. John offers advice and wisdom that men and women alike will appreciate since research on "gendered closeness" suggests that women and men both experience intimacy and closeness in their relationships[9].

Herein lies the book's greatest promise. It recognizes the duality of similarity and difference in men's and women's search for intimacy and addresses that issue directly. Intimacy is an important part of relationship satisfaction for both genders[10]. Indeed, Wood[11] argues that gender differences in communication are less pronounced than gender similarities. In other words, scholars[12] report that there are more similarities in what men and women want from close relationships than differences. For instance, "both sexes engage in both instrumental and expressive forms of caring, although each sex may emphasize some ways of expressing caring more than others. Both sexes like to feel needed and cherished, and both like to demonstrate cherishing to loved ones"[13].

However, despite our similarities, we tend to engage the world according to our own gendered standpoint[14]. For instance, women appear to define "closeness" in terms of depth or intimacy of disclosure[15]. Our experience tells us that men and women often struggle with relationship development and maintenance simply because we don't always operate from the same frame of reference. Instead, we operate within a mode that works for our own gender. In other words, men tend to treat women like other men and women's expectations for men are sometimes unrealistic. This leads to confusion, disappointment and perhaps even relational deterioration and dissolution. Relationships end before they even truly begin or have a chance to flourish. Mistakes are made because we simply don't know better. However, John clearly points out how men can stop making the same mistakes and get out of the downward spiral that often sends us into relationship purgatory. He offers concrete advice about how to stop making the same mistakes and, instead, try new approaches and techniques that actually work. This work recognizes important differences and fundamental similarities between women and men, helping men in search of intimacy navigate the often treacherous waters of negotiating a first date.

The benefits of a book such as this are insurmountable. Relationships are necessary, unavoidable, and essential to human beings. We need them to survive. But we need healthy relationships to thrive. Respecting differences and similarities creates an opportunity for a balanced view of how men and women seek intimacy through communication. If we are interested in mutual respect, meaningful forms of toleration, and the cultivation of civic forms of friendship that may lead to meaningful personal relationships, it is necessary to consider *humanitas* or the deepest dimensions of persons[16]. This book offers a balanced approach to intimacy and practical wisdom for seeking it.

Laurie J. Moroco, Ph.D.
Chair, Associate Professor
Department of Communication
Thiel College

Author's Notes

I am grateful to many people for helping me complete this book. Angelina, D'Arcy, Erica, Jamie, Kelley, Lisa (both of you), Michelle and Terry provided helpful feedback throughout the process.

Becky and Tom provided the original idea, which has long since been discarded.

Chris provided computer insight and advice.

Becky and Tom, Eric, Jasmine, Jim and my sister Carol for lending me money to finish the project. It's hard to write when you are constantly worried about money.

Kimberly Holtzman-Sloan provided me an unexpected opportunity to succeed.

Professor Janie M. Harden Fritz, Ph.D., Director of both the Undergraduate Program and Master of Arts Programs in the Department of Communication & Rhetorical Studies at Duquesne University for introducing me to Professor Kristin Roeschenthaler Wolfe.

Professor Wolfe has been a blessing. She understood immediately where I was going with the books. Her initial review of the material was a big help and led directly to reformatting the books and reordering the content.

Thanks,
John Gillies
Summer, 2009

Contents

Appendix

Introduction

"Give us the tools, and we will finish the job."
Sir Winston Churchill[17]

There is a very simple reason you are reading this book. Your social life is in disarray. Usually, you can't even get a date. On those rare occasions when you actually get a date, the date is a train wreck. You are ready to stop trying.

You have probably bought several "self-help" books in the past. You are probably suspicious of this book because it is so small and costs so much.

I have chosen to cut this book down to the bare bones. Most self-help books have page after page of mumbo-jumbo and psychobabble. You don't need to read these things, and you probably don't want to read them, so I intentionally left them out of the book.

Authors of self-help manuals often include examples that are pointless - and some are actually misleading. I have intentionally left out every example that was not absolutely necessary. Your mind will form images of people and places as you read the book. Use those images as your examples.

This book is blunt. It tells you what you are doing wrong; why it's wrong; the correct way to do it; and it has real-world exercises to enhance your skills and build your confidence. Some of the exercises may offend you or you may feel the exercise insults your intelligence. Please do them anyway. I have personally used every exercise in this book and they have worked for me.

As far as the price of this book goes, I urge you to change your perspective. Bad dates are very expensive.

Think of your last bad date and how much cash you wasted. Now consider how much money you will waste on your next bad date. Look at the price of this book as an investment in your future and your happiness. The rest of your life is worth more than the price of this book.

It's time you started living that way.

How to Use This Book

"Lather, rinse, repeat. . ."
Anonymous[18]

Read the chapter, do the exercises, write down what you did, write down your results, and then go on to the next chapter. It's simple and it works.

Your life begins where the book ends. After that, what you do is up to you.

Her Fear

> *"Reality is not the way you want things to be; Reality is not the way things appear to be; Reality is the way things actually ARE."*
>
> *Robert J. Ringer*[19]

Rape. Murder. Domestic violence.

You should not be surprised that a book about dating starts with a chapter about these things. Most dating books don't even mention them, but the abusive actions of a small percentage of men affect every interaction you have with women.

Violence against women is a huge problem. It is so big that I believe the following is true: A man has abused every woman you talk to or it has happened to one of her friends[20].

All communication takes place in context. Violence colors the context of male-female interactions. In other words, the violent, selfish actions of a few men have caused women to fear you simply because you are a man.

Is this fair? Who cares? Fairness is irrelevant. Women are reacting emotionally to a situation. They are afraid for their safety.

This is reality. Your ability to get dates, the dates you get, and your relationships will not improve until you accept this reality.

The actions of other men affect how women see you. This effect is almost entirely negative and causes women to fear you. To overcome the fear, you must set yourself apart from other men. The rest of this book is about setting yourself apart from other men. Each exercise helps you along that path.

Exercise # 1

Find a woman with whom you can talk candidly. Talk with her about this topic. Using the space below, analyze the conversation. What parts did you find valuable? What parts of the conversation made you uncomfortable?

Exercise # 2

Write down the next ten mass-media images you notice that involve violent acts committed by men against women. How long did it take you to finish this exercise? How does that make you feel?

Your Fear

> *"Fear has nothing to do with cowardice. A fellow is only yellow when he lets his fear make him quit."*
> *Jerome Cady*[21]

You probably have two primary fears. That she will reject you or that you will hurt her. Having these fears is normal and dealing with them is very straightforward.

Dealing With Your Fear of Hurting Women

> *"A woman is like a teabag - only in hot water do you realize how strong she is."*
> *Eleanor Roosevelt*[22]

Women are tougher than you think. If you do not:

1. commit violent acts against them;
2. lie to them;
3. steal from them; or
4. cheat on them;

then you cannot hurt them. You might do or say something stupid that will upset them. They might even break off the relationship. But it won't hurt them.

Exercise # 3
The next time you find yourself about to prevent a woman from doing something simply because she's a woman, immediately stop what you are doing. Apologize to the woman for your behavior, tell her you were being sexist or chauvinistic, and offer her the choice of doing it for herself or allowing you to do it for her.

Exercise # 4
Write down ten sexist things you have done. Did these behaviors affect your relationships with women? If so, was the effect positive or negative?

Dealing With Your Fear of Rejection

"Your piece stinks. We fed it to the turtle."
David Holahan[23]

Deal with it. You are going to get rejected. It has happened to you before and it's going to happen again.

Every man you know has been rejected more than once. Nobody cares except you and the only reason you care is because your brain is all messed up.

If you ask a woman for a date and she says "No," then you feel that the woman is rejecting you. This is incorrect. She doesn't even know you yet. It's just not possible for her to be rejecting you at this stage.

The woman simply declined to participate in an activity. There could be several reasons why she declined. She might already have a man in her life, or she might be getting over a bad relationship and isn't ready to date anyone right now.

"He conquers who endures."
Persius[24]

In some cases, it's possible her rejection might be temporary and she may well accept your advances next week or next month.

Take notes on your rejections. Save these notes because many of the women who gave vague or non-specific reasons will go out with you after you learn how to convert "No" into "Maybe" and eventually into "Yes."

Exercise # 5

Write down the details each time your request for a date or other activity is rejected by a woman. Get as much detail as possible and be very specific about the reason(s) she gave. Analyze the rejection. Did she give a unique reason that pertains to you? Or did she give you a non-specific reason?

What Kind of Woman and Relationship Do You Want?

> *"Everything is in the mind. That's where it all starts. Knowing what you want is the first step toward getting it."*
>
> *Mae West*[25]

Your social life is not going to improve until you decide what kind of woman you want and what kind of relationship you want. The most important aspect of these decisions is that they force you to focus your attention and resources on a smaller group of women.

You already know what your preferences are. You want a certain look, attitude, education, or lifestyle. You also know that you will probably be "unhappy" if you settle for less. The catch is that people are constantly changing. Your dream girl will be a completely different woman twenty years from now. You will be a different man as well.

It is impossible to make progress toward a goal unless you know what your goal is; therefore, the next few lessons focus on your wants and needs in this moment so that you can define some goals. The best result is where you find a woman that meets your needs and fuels your desires while you do the same thing for her. This might happen with the first woman you meet or the next woman you go on a date with, but the odds are against it.

Even if you follow every piece of advice in this book perfectly, you are still going to have bad dates. The point of these exercises is to increase your odds of finding a good relationship and decreasing the time it takes to do it.

Exercise # 6
Visualize your dream woman. Write a brief description (twenty-five words or less).

Exercise # 7
In 30 seconds or less, write down five aspects of your ideal woman's character or personality. The faster you go, the more honest you will be with yourself.

Exercise # 8
Write down what kind of relationship you want. Be general and be brief (twenty-five words or less).

What Sort of Man Are You?

> *"Men who cannot deceive others are very often successful at deceiving themselves."*
> *Samuel Johnson*[26]

In the previous chapter, you outlined the woman you want. You gave her a physical form and some personality attributes. You also described what kind of relationship you are looking for.

Now you must figure out whom you are and what you are going to contribute to the relationship. You must also figure out what baggage you are bringing into the relationship that might wreck it.

This exercise requires you to be diligent and completely honest with yourself. No one else will ever see the results. You already know the truth. Now is the time to face the truth so you can get on with your life. Look ahead at exercise #12.

Dating relationships always involve an exchange and are classic examples of "value for value relationships"†. You want something you value from the woman you are pursuing. She wants something she values from you; therefore, you have to know who you are and what you are bringing to the table.

Some of these values are purely physical, and they have a valid and important place in our lives; others are financial or emotional. Some are short-term and some take a long time to develop. The important point is to identify what kinds of needs you have and what kind of needs you can fulfill.

---

† From **MILLION DOLLAR HABITS**, Robert J. Ringer (1990) Fawcett

Exercise # 9
Take some pictures of yourself. Determine what you bring to the table physically. List two things you want to change over time. Find five positive things about your body.

Exercise # 10
In sixty seconds or less, list your five best personal qualities.

Exercise # 11
In sixty seconds or less, list five personal qualities that are most likely to wreck the relationship.

Personal Preparations

> *"Be prepared."*
> *Boy Scout Motto*

Your character, bearing, posture, body language, grooming, clothing and your environment must all be properly prepared before you venture out to meet women. It would be a terrible waste if you happened upon a wonderful woman, but you were unable to seal the deal because one of these areas had been left unattended.

Character

> *"Always tell the truth. That way, you don't have to remember anything."*
> *Mark Twain*[27]

From this point forward, you must be honest and forthright in your dealings. If you prove to the women in your life that you can be trusted, then you will have overcome their fear. The best way to build trust is simply by being honest. Honesty cannot be faked, nor can you be honest part of the time. Therefore, lying to women just to get dates or have sex is no longer permitted.

You must also be sincere when dealing with people. No more patronizing people, no more fake smiles, and no more emotional masks. Insincerity is form of lying and you must eliminate it from your life before you go on to the next chapter.

From this point forward, you should deal in facts and truths, resolve issues based on those realities, and accept the consequences of your actions.

For many of you, the exercise for this chapter will cause you A LOT of emotional pain. Do it anyway.

Exercise # 12

If you are in a conversation and catch yourself telling a lie you, must stop the conversation and immediately apologize for lying to the person. Then you must tell the person the truth. Finally, you must accept the consequences of your action.

Here's an example apology:

"I'm sorry. I just lied to you about ________. I should not have lied because you deserve the truth. What really happened is __________. Please accept my apology. I won't do that to you again."

You will probably need to modify the example to fit your personal style and the circumstances. Write down the details of the conversation. You will probably discover that you lie about stupid things for no reason.

Bearing

"Ev'ry mornin' at the mine you could see him arrive,
He stood six foot six and weighed two forty five,
Kinda broad at the shoulder and narrow at the hip,
And everybody knew ya didn't give no lip to Big John."

Jimmy Dean[28]

Your bearing is the overall effect of your appearance. The whole should be more than the sum of the parts[29]. Bearing includes grooming and clothing, but it also includes how you carry yourself.

In simple terms, bearing is the visual component of leadership.

Posture

"I grow, I prosper;
Now, Gods, stand up for bastards!"

William Shakespeare[30]

Your posture and bearing always make a statement, but you are probably making the wrong statement. You probably have the posture and bearing of a follower. Women don't want guys who settle for second.

Proper posture involves your whole body. Your legs should be vertical, with your feet directly below your hips. Your arms should hang easily at your sides and should sway effortlessly as you walk. Your neck is relaxed and your chin should be level to the ground. Your head should be centered above your body.

Exercise # 13
Rent Bridge on the River Kwai. Watch how Colonel Nicholson marches and walks. Even after being tortured, he attempts to maintain his posture and his bearing. Emulate how he carries himself when he is physically healthy.

Medical Note: *If either standing upright or walking properly cause pain, get to a doctor or chiropractor to have a medical professional figure out why it hurts.*

Body Language

"Nice move. Did you make that up?"
Stephanie Mangano[31]

Your posture is probably sending the signal that you are a follower. The rest of your body language tells the world what kind of follower you are. The way you carry your arms and legs, how you sit and how you move tells the world you are a bitter loser, groveling toady or a star-struck fool. You are probably none of those things, but your body language is sending the wrong signals.

Leaders have a very well developed set of postures and positions. Leaders tend to be calm and still, rarely shifting or fidgeting. Women gravitate to men who look and act like leaders and subconsciously avoid men who look and act like "second bananas."

In general, leaders are relaxed at all times. Leaders make themselves comfortable and available. This means you should always sit with proper posture while allowing others to approach you easily and without obstruction.

When moving, move at a relaxed pace. Keep your motions smooth.

You should avoid crossing your arms because this position sends negative messages like boredom or anger[32]. Similarly, you should avoid sitting behind desks or tables because these physical objects often become psychological obstacles to communications.

Exercise # 14
Find a place where you can sit undisturbed in front of a mirror. Get comfortable in front of the mirror without crossing your arms or legs. Get used to that pose. Train yourself to sit that way every time you go out.

Exercise # 15
Stand undisturbed in front of a mirror for about one minute. Do not become tense or "stand at attention." Work on maintaining good posture while standing. When you do move, define your motions down and make each motion count. *Do not fidget!* You can combine this exercise with daily grooming for variety.

Hands

"Good hands."
Bob Uecker[33]

You are probably using your hands without even noticing it. You could be doing anything mindlessly with your hands from peeling the label off your beer bottle to constantly primping and preening.

The human eye instinctively follows motion. Women cannot concentrate on you if your hands are constantly distracting them by moving and fiddling too much.

There is a correct method to keep your hands relaxed when not in use. Do not shove your hands into your pockets, fold them in your lap, or stand around with your hands on your hips. Just relax your arms and allow your hands to come to rest naturally.

This next exercise addresses the issue of hand movement in a context that is very important if you are looking for a long-term relationship involving children. Women notice if you are unable to cook for yourself. This is big issue for many women. A woman will assume that if you can't cook for yourself, you will not be able to cook for her kids. If you are looking for a long-term relationship, you will have to deal with domestic issues like cooking and childcare.

Exercise # 16

Cook for yourself at least three times a week. Cook an actual meal that requires using real dishes. Simple meals that come out of boxes are OK, but using the microwave to cook dinner DOES NOT COUNT! The meal must have a beverage and at least three different items. The beverage must be served in a glass WITHOUT a straw and all of the items must require you to use silverware to eat them.

Eat the meal at a relaxed pace using proper table manners during the entire meal (chew your food with your mouth closed, put your silverware down while chewing, and keep your elbows off the table)[34].

The object is for you to notice what your hands are doing while you are chewing your food. Your hands should be resting comfortably on the armrests of the chair if it has them or on top of your thighs if it does not.

Over time, your hands will become calm when not in use. As an added bonus, you will improve your cooking and table manners.

Feet

"I've got ...happy feet!"
Steve Martin[35]

And you won't be getting anywhere if you do. Feet are very similar to hands because you can be moving them without knowing you are doing it. Shifting your weight from foot to foot is the most common issue.

Motion is distracting, so every time you shuffle your feet you direct the woman's attention away from you and to your feet. Then you have to get her attention again and the whole cycle repeats.

Constantly moving your feet also implies you are waiting for the signal to go somewhere. Leaders do not wait for signals; they give signals. Leaders do not shuffle and shift, they stand calmly until it's time to move - and then they move with a purpose.

Medical Note: ***If you are shifting from foot to foot because you are physically uncomfortable, then there may be an underlying medical condition. One of your legs may be longer than the other or your hips might be out of alignment. If you think this is the case, get to a doctor or chiropractor and have a professional check you out. These are common medical issues and can usually be resolved quickly and cheaply.***

Exercise # 17

Go to any pet store and buy a couple of cheap cat toys - the little balls with the bells in them. Tie these to your shoes. Make notes every time the bells ring and you are not actually walking from place to place. Also, make a note of every time you walk around without having a specific purpose.

Do the exercise at home when you are alone. If you do this exercise in public two bad things happen: the bells annoy people and you look like a dork.

You might think this is a stupid exercise. You only have to do this exercise a few times, so just deal with it.

Eye Contact

"Look into my eyes!"
Svengali[36]

You have to make eye contact with women if you are going to get anywhere with them. You will build trust, confidence, and credibility by looking her in the eye when it's appropriate. Staring at your shoes sends the message that you are weak. Avoiding eye contact indicates you might have something to hide. It just won't work. You must look women in the eye because in many important ways women expect you to be the leader.

You should look women in the eyes every time you talk to them. Keep it short at first. Don't let your eyes linger after the conversation tapers off. Eventually, the eye contact will naturally continue into the silence. Eye contact is part of the "unspoken communication" that occurs during a conversation. The frequency and duration of eye contact will change as you become more familiar with the woman. How the woman reacts to this prolonged eye contact is a strong indicator of how well or poorly you are doing.

A word of caution here: Don't stare! This is not a contest to determine who will blink first. This is a serious step in the courtship process. You definitely want to have frequent eye contact, but you don't want to linger too long because it may make the woman feel uncomfortable.

Maintaining eye contact is the single most important element in setting up a first kiss with a woman. That's in the next book.

Exercise # 18

Get dressed in front of the mirror every day. Use the mirror to get dressed. Do not look at your clothes unless you have to. Make it a point to look yourself in the eye periodically as you get dressed. Gradually extend the time you look into your own eyes.

Grooming

"A dog's idea of personal grooming is to roll in a dead fish."

James Gorman[37]

Grooming is more than just shaving, showering, and brushing your teeth. Those things are simple cleaning.

Grooming means paying attention to the details and doing the "little things." Women notice this stuff and they care about it. It's time for another field trip. This time you're going to the salon. I prefer full service salons like Aveda and "The Art of Shaving," but you can go wherever you like.

You are going to get four things done at the salon. This trip will be pricey, but the stylists and beauticians will teach you what to do. You will do most of your own work in the future to save some cash.

The minimum salon activities list:

1. Haircut
2. Manicure and pedicure
3. Hair removal
4. Supplies

Haircut: This item is especially important if you are losing your hair. Bring along some photos of other men with haircuts that you like and ask the stylist if she thinks the style in the picture would be good for you. If you have a comb-over or a toupee, it's time to get rid of it. Why? Combovers and toupees are signs of weakness and vanity. They are also a form of lying (see exercise #12).

Manicure and pedicure: Pay attention to what the nail professionals are doing. You want to duplicate the results when you trim your own nails. Women notice if your fingernails are jagged or dirty.

Hair removal: Have an aesthetician go over your ears, eyebrows and nose to remove any excess hairs or hairs that look out of place. This is not much fun for the aesthetician, so be sure to tip heavily.

Supplies: Buy a bottle of every product that was used on you. Use them at home. This DOES NOT mean you are a metrosexual. It means you are considering the desires of women when you groom yourself.

Exercise # 19

How was your trip to the salon? Did you tell the stylist why you were there? What advice did she give you? Are you comfortable with it? Write down your impressions, feelings and your intended course of action. Take some pictures of yourself. Take notes on what works for you and what you need to change next time around.

Exercise # 19
(continued)

Clothing

> *"If I saw myself dressed like that, I'd have to kick my own ass."*
>
> *Adam Sandler*[38]

Your clothes are the first message you send to the women you are pursuing. You are probably sending all the wrong messages with your wardrobe. The first thing women notice about your clothes is cleanliness, followed by appropriateness, quality, fit, style, and condition.

If you choose to upgrade your wardrobe, there are two great places to get guidance. The best place is from women, especially from the women that meet your criteria for a long-term relationship. Another place to look for guidance is women's magazines. This might seem odd, but consider this: The men pictured on these pages are there specifically because they appeal to women. These men demonstrate how to dress and behave. This is especially true for the men in the *advertisements* on these pages.

Keeping your clothes clean is mandatory. Women understand clothes are expensive and will tolerate clothes that are a bit dated, but they will not tolerate clothes that are dirty. This is especially important if you work with chemicals or solvents that have peculiar odors that could be accidentally transferred to the woman's clothing.

Tip: If you think it's dirty, then it's dirty.

Exercise # 20

This exercise has to wait until you are done with Basic Research. Find a picture of a man in one of those magazines. How close is your look to his? Can you dress like he does with your current wardrobe? Do you need some new clothes? Write your results here.

Exercise # 21

Go through your clothes and get rid of everything you have not worn in the last six months. The clothes that are in good repair (or that can be easily repaired) should be donated to charity. Throw the others away. Write down what you did and how long it took.

Exercise # 22

Ask a woman you know to go through your closet with you. Ask her to evaluate your clothes. Determine what works for you, what does not, and what you need to add to your wardrobe. Write your notes here.

Your Environment

"Dennis! There's some lovely filth down here!"
Woman[39]

Messy homes and cars turn off most women. The best case scenario is that the mess in your home distracts them. The worst case scenario is that it gives the woman an excuse to dump you.

If a woman dumps you because you cannot clean up after yourself, she will tell every woman she knows what a slob you are. Your reputation as a slob will make it harder for you to get dates with women in this social group.

If you are thinking about having kids, then the women you will be dating are probably thinking about having kids as well. One thought that will cross her mind is, "How will he be able to clean up after the kids if he can't even clean out his car?" Excessive messiness is a deal-breaker in these cases.

If you cannot afford to keep your car clean, then you cannot afford a girlfriend.

Exercise # 23

Get all the crap out of your car. Your vehicle should not double as a garbage scow. Fast-food wrappers on the passenger seat are NOT sexy. Get your car cleaned. Most of us cannot afford the $125 for a professional detailing, but you should drop $20 for a decent car wash where the interior gets vacuumed.

Exercise # 24

Invite one of your friends over and ask him to bring his girlfriend. Ask her to evaluate your apartment's cleanliness. Ask her which things are "deal breakers" that must be corrected before you invite a woman into your home. Do what she tells you to do. Hire professionals if you have to.

Where to Find Women

"You got to be careful if you don't know where you're going, because you might not get there."
Yogi Berra[40]

According to legend, Willie Sutton robbed banks because that's where the money was. You should follow Willie's example and go to where the women are.

Women's magazines have articles that tell women where to go to meet men. Even obscure magazines about vegetarianism or yoga will occasionally have articles about dating and finding "that special someone."

Some of these articles will actually tell you where to go, for example: "The best places to meet single men are..." Go where the magazine says you are supposed to be.

There is also a counter-intuitive approach to finding women. Go to where there are no men (or very few men). You can't get into *Curves*™, but you can find places where there will be more women than men. You will need to be creative and resourceful for this method to be effective. This method also requires you to have a thick skin. You need a thick skin because some of the women in these places are actively avoiding men and your presence will disturb them.

It is impossible to offer even general advice on where to go for the counter-intuitive method. Local culture and conditions have a tremendous impact on this method. Techniques that work in big cities are probably not going to work very well in small towns. Likewise, things that work in landlocked farming towns may not work manufacturing centers and ports.

Exercise # 25

Go to a bookstore that has a large, well-stocked magazine section. Find women's magazines that have pictures of your dream woman on the cover. Check the table of contents. Do the articles reflect the values and relationship goals you outlined in the previous chapters? If not, put that magazine aside.

If the table of contents looks promising, then it's time to dig deeper. Look for the articles about dating, socializing, and romance. These articles will tell you where the women you want are looking for you.

You will probably want to repeat this exercise. You may need to modify this exercise if you live in a sparsely populated area or an area that does not have many bookstores.

Scouting Missions

"I find that a great part of the information I have was acquired by looking up something and finding something else on the way."
Franklin P. Adams[41]

At this point, you have done some research, worked on your grooming and character, cleaned your home, and even de-junked your car. You are probably tempted to just jump right in and start pursuing the woman of your dreams.

Don't do it!

You've been alone and lonely for a long time. Of course there is a strong desire to end your dry spell immediately.

Be patient for just a little longer. Invest a few days scouting out the best places to meet women.

A "Normal" Day

"You can observe a lot just by watching."
Yogi Berra

You probably think that there are no single women in your life. This is false. You just have not noticed them. Even on the most ordinary day, many women cross your path. Many of them are single and you can probably get dates with several of them if you play your cards right.

What has happened is you have gotten into a rut that prevents you from noticing them. Why you got there is unimportant. You need to start noticing these women. Doing this will bring pleasure for its own sake and will snap you out of your rut.

Exercise # 26

Do not change your routine to do this exercise. Every time you interact with a woman, make a note of where it happened. Any interaction counts, even things as small as you waved at her and she waved back, as long as it was an actual interaction. Remember that you are recording the *place*, not the *woman*. Do this and record your results.

Pretty soon, you will have a list of places where there are women who will interact with you.

Research Directed

"If you want be a party animal, you have to learn to live in the jungle."

Lisa[42]

Your initial research revealed several places where you can go to meet the kind of women you are looking for.

It's time to go. You might have a little stage fright when doing this exercise, BUT leave immediately if you feel something is really wrong. You can always come back later. It's better to walk away too early than to stick around too long and screw up.

You might be in strange circumstances, in unfamiliar places, or doing new things. These things aren't as bad as they seem. Don't let your fear or shyness wreck this for you. You can actually use your lack of knowledge and experience as a conversation starter (see exercise 36 through 39 for some hints).

Exercise # 27

Get cleaned up and dressed properly. Go to the places your research indicated the women you want would be looking for you. Calmly observe what is happening. Ask yourself the important questions: Are the women here? Are they what I am looking for? Do I look like I belong here? Am I dressed correctly?

If the answer to all these questions is "Yes" then go ahead and pat yourself on the back. You have hit the jackpot and are in the right spot. There's no need to do anything else yet. Spend a few minutes browsing and observing. Make note of what is happening. Chalk up this trip as a victory. Move on to check out some more locations. You'll be back here tomorrow.

If the answer to any of these questions is "No," exit quickly and quietly. Re-evaluate your research and correct the bad item(s).

The Best Women to Find

"A man chases a woman until she catches him."
American Proverb

The best women to find are the ones that are looking for a man. The best place to find them is online. There are many dating sites on the Internet. Investigating these sites is in your best interest. The women who use these sites have done a bunch of work for you.

Now it's your turn to do some work. The work is not hard, but it does take a while. Before you begin searching dating sites you need to do exercises 28 and 29.

"Flesh and blood needs flesh and blood and you're the one I need."
Johnny Cash[43]

The best women on Internet dating sites are the ones who have paid for the service and have posted a picture. You can assume these women are real and are serious about finding a man.

This is not a guarantee of success. It does not mean you are going to meet someone today, start dating tomorrow, and be having a Las Vegas wedding officiated by an Elvis impersonator next weekend. It does increase your chances of finding fun, interesting women and getting some high quality dates.

The corollary to this rule is that these women are not even going to consider you unless you post a picture and pay for the service.

Do not subscribe to or pay for anything yet. Go on line and inspect five dating sites. You are looking for three important things:

1. How many local women have paid for the service;
2. How many local women have paid for the service;
3. How many local women have paid for the service?

That's not a typo. Are enough women from your area on this site to make it worth your time and money? The site might be pretty, easy to use and have great advertising. So what? If there are no local women who are offering what you want and want what you've got, then it isn't worth your time.

Remember: **Dating is a numbers game.** Increasing the number of women you interact with is the best way to get the dates and ultimately the relationship you are looking for. It's also a numbers game in that you want to reduce the number of bad dates you have by filtering out women that are not a good match for you.

Exercise # 28

Get at least three and preferably five images of yourself. These should be in .jpg format and slightly larger than passport photos. Wear different a different shirt in each picture. One or two should include a prop from your hobby and another one should include other people. Choose wisely, because these pictures will eventually become part of your on line profile. One picture should be new and taken when you are at your best. Proper grooming is a must for all of these images. It's OK to ask for help or to hire a photographer to make certain you have a good picture.

Exercise # 29

Refer back to exercises 10 & 11. Build those two exercises into an exciting paragraph that describes you. Write in the first person and use active verbs. Use a spell checker and a grammar checker. This is going to be the basis for your profile.

Exercise # 30

This is going to be an important part of your profile.

Refer back to exercises 7 & 8. Build those two exercises into a short story that describes the woman you are looking for. As in exercise #29, write in the first person; use active verbs and future tense. Check and re-check your spelling and grammar.

Exercise # 31
Go to at least five different dating websites. Write down the name of each site and how many local women with paid profiles were available on it.

Exercise # 32
Pick the Internet dating site with the most available local women with paid for profiles and sign up. Put your best foot forward. Use the best pictures you have available. CHECK YOUR WORK! There should be NO typos or grammatical errors in your profile.

Exercise # 33
Once your profile is active and the photos are available for the world to see, it's time to contact every local woman with a paid for profile that appeals to you on that site. Keep your initial contact short, refer to her profile in every response, and do not use "cut and paste" to write or edit your responses. Women can tell when you "cut and paste" your responses. In general, women do not like "cut and paste" responses and usually do not respond to them.

Keep track of your results.

Preparations Part Two

> *"Perfection is achieved, not when there is nothing more to add, but when there is nothing left to take away."*
>
> *Antoine de Saint Exupery*[44]

Always have a plan for what you would do on a first date ready to go before you leave the house. Your first date plan should be short and sweet. It needs to include:

1. one or two times that you are available; and
2. the location that you want to go to; and
3. an activity; and
4. the approximate cut off time.

You must have this information available **right now**. When you ask a woman out, she assumes you have a plan. If you don't have a plan she will think you are just another loser who cannot make a decision and only wants her for sex.

Having a plan puts you in charge even if your plan is bad or stupid. Your plan should roll off your tongue easily in one simple sentence. "Let's do (activity) at (place) on (time)." This initial activity should be something public, relatively inexpensive, and non-threatening.

This is a first date, so your suggestions should be low-key and involve a lot of conversation. Avoid situations that restrict conversations, are centered on alcohol consumption, or are highly sexualized.

There will be gaps in your conversation during the date. This is normal, but many people freeze up during these times. Doing something during the date helps fill these gaps and is the primary reason why step #3 is included in the plan.

The cut off time is handy diagnostic tool. If you and your date are both having fun when the cut-off time arrives, you can just keep going. If you are not having fun, then the cut-off time becomes an "escape hatch." Item #4 is included because some dates just don't work out.

You should have a couple of alternate plans available in case your primary plan falls through due to an unforeseen circumstance like a freak change in the weather.

Exercise # 34
Plan a first date. Follow the "Let's do (activity) at (place) on (time)" model.

Exercise # 35
Rehearse asking an imaginary woman on this date. Do your rehearsals in front of a mirror.
Rehearse until the details are locked firmly in your memory.

Flirting

"Wait Master, it might be dangerous... you go first."

Igor[45]

The big mistake most men make is that they do not attempt to flirt enough. Some men skip opportunities to flirt, other men will only flirt with one woman at a time, and some men refuse to flirt at all.

You are reading this book, so you are probably single and available. Flirting is a safe and harmless way to advertise your availability.

There are some small downsides to flirting. You may put your foot in your mouth, or you may try to flirt with a woman who is having a bad day and reacts poorly. These events are going to be rare and should not discourage you.

Usually, you will brighten someone's day and nothing more will come of it. This is OK because spreading good cheer is a noble result in and of itself. And you might just stumble across a good relationship.

Increase Your Interactions with Women

"How interesting. I have a husband named Dean Wormer at Faber. Still want to show me your cucumber?"

Marion Wormer[46]

The single best way to meet more women is to slow down. If you are like most men, then you are trying to do things too fast. This may make you feel like you are really "getting things done," but it prevents single women from interacting with you.

Slowing the pace of your life is a pretty big change. You will need to slow the pace of your life in the future because girlfriends and relationships require time commitments. Do it now so you become used to it.

Exercise # 36
Skip drive-through lanes. Banks, pharmacies, dry cleaners, and restaurants all still have inside service. Park your car, walk inside, and talk to the person that works there. You can probably arrange it so you will be talking to a woman. Pay her a compliment and chat for a few moments.

Exercise # 37
Identify another way to increase the number of women you come into contact with every day.

Simple Compliments

> *"A man who would move a mountain begins with very small stones."*
>
> *Chinese proverb*

The mistake you are probably making is that you take people for granted. When you do, you ignore common courtesies. The result is that you appear cold, heartless, and crass. This is the smallest step, but it's also the first step. If you don't do this, then nothing else can follow.

The simple compliment comes naturally and is basically just an acknowledgment of the woman. This can be a simple thank you after she hands you your change or a quick, pleasant remark about her hairstyle or her shoes.

Exercise # 38

Think of some women whom you interacted with recently but did not take time to compliment. Write down simple compliments you could have given to them.

Activity Flirting

> *"There are times not to flirt: When you're sick. When you're with children. When you're on the witness stand."*
>
> *Joyce Jillson*[47]

You have now identified what kind of woman you want in your life, what kind of man you are, and have a pretty good idea where to find the woman of your dreams. These are good things.

It's time for a simple, practical exercise. It's time for some flirting. For this exercise, you will pay a compliment to a woman you do not know. The compliment must be for something the woman does, not for her appearance.

The goal here is for you to do the exercise several times a day and to do it flawlessly. You are not going to do this exercise until you get it right. You are going to practice this exercise until you cannot get it wrong.

Paying honest and sincere compliments to people who deserve them is going to become part of you.

The compliment will come in three parts:

1. Acknowledging the woman's presence; and
2. Acknowledging what she did; and finally
3. Telling her why it was special.

You could offer the compliment at the bank, at a restaurant, or even during a phone call.

Exercise # 39

Pay a compliment to a woman you do not know. The compliment must be for something the woman did. You must be honest and sincere. Keep track of the compliments you give to people. Include as many details as you can.

Body Flirting

> *"A lot of guys think the larger a woman's breasts are, the less intelligent she is. I don't think it works like that. I think it's the opposite. I think the larger a woman's breasts are, the less intelligent men become."*
>
> *Anita Wise*[48]

In this section, you are going to flirt by paying women compliments about their physical appearance. You are going to do this on a regular basis. You are going to practice every day.

Body flirting is the equal of Activity Flirting, and whichever type of flirting you use is based on how you feel at the time.

You must be very careful when body flirting. If you say the wrong thing or compliment the wrong body part, you could alienate the woman you are flirting with. In general, you want to compliment some aspect of the woman's appearance that she controls directly and that she can change with relative ease.

Study the photograph on the back cover. Practice complimenting women on the items listed in green print on the picture.

Avoid the areas marked "No!" in large red boxes. The teller at the bank might have a lovely cleavage; the cocktail waitress might have a firm and shapely rear end. Don't stare! Women have very little control over the size and shape of their bust, their legs or their rear end. Compliments regarding these areas are appropriate later in the relationship. At this point in the relationship you should simply compose yourself, look her in the eyes and pay her an honest compliment about some other aspect of her appearance.

Complimenting a woman on her appearance is easy. It's very similar to the Activity Compliment from the last chapter and has three parts:

1. Acknowledging the woman's presence; and
2. Telling her which part of her appearance pleases you; and finally
3. Explaining what you noticed about it.

Once again, there will be no examples. Develop your own "signature compliment." Most of all, you should be original. You should learn to think on your feet and give these compliments freely and easily.

Exercise # 40

Think of some women whom you saw recently. Write down simple compliments about their appearance.

Exercise # 41

Pay a compliment to a woman you do not know. The compliment must be for the woman's appearance. It must be something she controls (clothing and accessories are good places to start). You must be honest and sincere.

Multi-Session Flirting

> *"Tune in tomorrow! Same Bat-time! Same Bat-Channel!"*
>
> *William Dozier*[49]

You should be developing light, flirty relationships with the women you deal with on a routine basis. Developing these relationships builds and hones the skills you will need to get the dates you want. Additionally, one of these women might just turn into your girlfriend.

You probably have several places you go to on a regular basis: the bank, the gym, the coffee shop, and so on. There are plenty of women who work in these places and you can flirt with them over a period of weeks and months. They are probably not what you are looking for in terms of a partner. So what? You should still flirt with them on a regular basis.

You probably have some issues like fear of rejection, or fear of failure, or any one of a number of neuroses. It's OK; nobody's perfect and everybody has some 'baggage'.

Developing a "working friendship" with the coffee lady or the letter carrier is a good way for you to identify your imperfections, determine what kind of baggage you have, and build your confidence.

Exercise # 42

Identify three women whom you see on a daily basis and with whom you have not interacted before. These women can be ANYBODY. You do not have to be sexually attracted to them. Start an ongoing friendly-flirty relationship with them. Your goal is to learn two simple but harmless facts about them within the next month.

Multi-Step Flirting

"I hope, for your sake, you were initiating a mating ritual."

B'Etor[50]

This is the part of flirting that is most interesting. This is where things come together. You should probably not even start this type of flirting until you can easily engage in both Activity Flirting and Body Flirting.

Once you are ready, you should engage in this type of flirting whenever possible because this type of flirting is the lead-in to asking for dates, and eventually dates lead to the relationship you want in your life.

Multi-Step Flirting involves the lead-in and the hook. The lead-in is either activity flirting or body flirting. The hook is a question or statement that provokes a positive response. The goal is to get the woman involved (hooked) in some sort of ongoing interaction with you.

Once the woman is on the hook, you just keep adding positive hooks until either you run out of hooks or you feel it's time to ask for a date. It looks like this:

1. Acknowledge the woman's presence; and
2. Acknowledge what she did or what she's wearing;
3. Tell her why it was special;
4. Ask a question about it;
5. Paraphrase her response and repeat it back to her;
6. Ask a question about her response.
    a. (repeat steps 5 and 6 as needed)
7. Decision:
    a. Ask for a date; or
    b. Leave gracefully

You can go back and forth to whatever kind of flirting works during the conversation. The conversation will almost never go in a straight line. There will be portions of the conversation where you are just talking about “things” and the conversation may not seem to be going where you want it to go. This is OK - just make sure to get back on track if you decide you want to ask this woman for a date. If you decide this woman is not going to work out, these “fillers” are an excellent time to let the conversation die off.

This will not always work. Some women are just not into you. It happens. Just as you are looking for a certain type of woman, she is looking for a certain type of man.

Exercise # 43

Get out there and do it, man! Make the effort and get all the way through this process. What did you choose at step 7? Did you make a decision? Did you ask for the date? Why or why not? If you asked for the date did you get it?

Asking for a Date

"I was thinking, maybe we could get some beer."
Pinto[51]

In football, the first points of the game are usually the hardest to get. With women, the first date is usually the hardest one to get and the easiest one to screw up. You already have a plan (see exercise #34). It's very basic, but it's enough.

When you ask for a date, do just exactly that. Ask. Nothing more and nothing less. Don't get emotional, poetic, bombastic, or whiny. "Let's go out" is perfectly acceptable, as is the format from exercise #34.

Exercise # 44

Write down exactly how you asked for the date. Did it work? Were you a leader when you asked? Or were you a groveling beggar?

The First Date

"Brevity is the soul of wit."
William Shakespeare[52]

Your first date plan should be a short date. Plan for about three hours, but leave extra time at the end of the date. Ideally, you should clear your calendar. Some first dates become extended dates and some even lead directly to romance and relationships.

"Another Saturday, another date.
She would be ready but she always makes them wait.
In the hallway, in anticipation,
He didn't know the night would end up in frustration.
He'd end up blowing all his wages for the week
All for a cuddle and a peck on the cheek."
The Kinks[53]

Another thing to plan for is what you are willing to spend on the first date. Leave yourself a margin of error, but don't go overboard. Allocating your money for a first date is very similar to going to the casino or the races: You shouldn't do it if you can't afford to lose it.

"Day, n. A period of twenty-four hours, mostly misspent."
Ambrose Bierce[54]

If you are enjoying yourself, your date is probably having a good time as well. Ask her if she wants to keep going.

This is an excellent time to hand her the reins and see what happens. If you have come to a point where you can logically end your planned date and segue into something else, give her a shot at it. Ask her what she wants to do now. If she doesn't have an answer, suggest one of your contingency plans from exercises 34 and 35.

Above all else, be willing to scrap your entire plan if the circumstances warrant. Your objective is to find a girlfriend. Don't lose sight of that. Think on your feet, take reasonable risks, and be willing to compromise.

Exercise # 45

What's your first date plan? How much extra time can you spend if you want to? How flexible can you be? Have you kept your costs in line?

Crash and Burn

"It's just a flesh wound."
The Black Knight[55]

Sometimes, things go "boom!" It happens. Write down what went wrong, why you think it went wrong and how you can prevent it next time.

Afterword

> *"Somewhere over the rainbow*
> *Skies are blue*
> *And the dreams that you dare to dream*
> *Really do come true."*
> *Dorothy Gale*[56]

The book's over.

There are no more quotes, or instructions, or exercises. Now it's on you. It's time to decide.

The rest of your life is waiting.

Appendix

Notes from the Foreword:

1. From **INTIMATE RELATIONSHIPS** by Sharon Brehm. Published in 1985 by McGraw-Hill.

2. Montgomery, B. (1988). **QUALITY COMMUNICATION IN PERSONAL RELATIONSHIPS**. In S Duck (Ed.), *Personal relationships: Theory, research, and interventions* (pp. 343-359). New York: Sage.

3. Parks, M., & Floyd, K. (1996). Meaning for closeness and intimacy in friendship. *Journal of Social and Personal Relationships, 13*(1), 85-107.

4. Sennett, R. (1977). **THE FALL OF PUBLIC MAN**. New York: Vintage.

5. Wiess, R. (1973). **LONELINESS: THE EXPERIENCE OF EMOTIONAL AND SOCIAL ISOLATION**. Cambridge, MA: MIT Press.

6. Rubin, L. (1973). **LIKING AND LOVING: AN INVITATION TO SOCIAL PSYCHOLOGY**. New York: Holt, Rinehart & Winston.

7. Hook, M., Gerstein, L., Detterich, L., & Gridley, B. (2003). How close are we? Measuring intimacy and examining gender. *Journal of counseling and development: JCD., 81*(4), 462-472.

8. Hook, M., Gerstein, L., Detterich, L., & Gridley, B. (2003). How close are we? Measuring intimacy and examining gender. *Journal of counseling and development: JCD., 81*(4), 462-472.

9. Wood, J., & Inman, C. (1993). In a different mode: Masculine styles of communicating closeness. *Journal of Applied Communication Research, 21*, 279-295.

10. Sprecher, S. & Hendrick, S. (2004). Self-disclosure in intimate relationships: Associations with individual and relationship characteristics over time. *Journal of Social and Clinical Psychology, 23*(6), 857-878.

11. Wood, J (2002). A critical response to John Gray's Mars and Venus portrayals of men and women. *Southern Communication Journal, 67*(2), 201-210.

12. Parks, M., & Floyd, K. (1996). Meaning for closeness and intimacy in friendship. *Journal of Social and Personal Relationships, 13*(1), 85-107, and

Vangelisti, A., & Daly, J. (1997). Gender differences in standards for romantic relationships. *Personal Relationships, 4,* 203-219.

13. Vangelisti, A., & Daly, J. (1997). Gender differences in standards for romantic relationships. *Personal Relationships, 4,* 205

14. Harding, S. (1991). **WHOSE SCIENCE? WHOSE KNOWLEDGE? THINKING FROM WOMEN'S LIVES** Ithaca: Cornell University Press.

15. Wood, J., & Inman, C. (1993). In a different mode: Masculine styles of communicating closeness. *Journal of Applied Communication Research, 21*, 279-295.

16. Button, M. (2005, April). "Arendt, Rawls, and Public Reason." *Social Theory & Practice, 31*,(2), 257-280.

Notes from the Text and Quotations:

17. This quote is from Winston Churchill's radio broadcast delivered in London in February 9, 1941. In January of that year, Wendell Willkie visited Britain. Willkie delivered a letter of introduction from President Roosevelt to Prime Minister Churchill. Roosevelt's letter included several quotations from Longfellow, and this letter greatly influenced Churchill's speech.

18. There were just so many choices for this quote. Sears hairdryers come with the advice "do not use while sleeping", many brands of Christmas lights advise us that they are for "indoor or outdoor use only" and a Swedish chainsaw manufacturer advises us "do not attempt to stop the chain with your hands or your genitals".

19. From Robert J. Ringer's best-selling book **WINNING THROUGH INTIMIDATION** which was originally written and self-published in 1973. The book has been substantially rewritten and is back in print as **TO BE OR NOT TO BE INTIMIDATED? THAT IS THE QUESTION**. I strongly urge you to read this book, as well as his two more of his books, **LOOKING OUT FOR # 1** and **MILLION DOLLAR HABITS**.

20. This assumes every woman you know has at least five female friends. Studies on the prevalence of domestic violence suggest that from one-fifth to one-third of all women will be physically assaulted by a partner or ex-partner during their lifetime. (Council on Scientific Affairs, American Medical Association. 1991. "Violence Against Women: Relevance for Medical Practitioners." Journal of the American Medical Association 267(23): 1992.)

21. Dialogue spoken by Captain Ross (Dana Andrews) in the movie **THE PURPLE HEART** (1944). The screenplay was written by Jerome Cady and Lewis Milestone. There were thousands of choices for this quote. Other possibilities included the *St. Crispin's Day Speech* from William Shakespeare's **HENRY V** or any of half a dozen choices from Christopher Marlowe's **TAMBURLAINE**.

22. There is a great deal of myth surrounding this quote. At various times it has been attributed to Mae West, Babe

Didrikson, Eleanor Roosevelt, Margaret Thatcher, Nancy Reagan and even Yogi Berra. Eleanor Roosevelt's 1960 book **YOU LEARN BY LIVING** has a written reference, so she gets the nod.

23. From the article: **DINING ON CARDBOARD AU GRATIN: A FREE-LANCER'S LAMENT**, originally published in the Christian Science Monitor, February 13, 1985.

24. Persius was very familiar with failure. He spent many years in exile because he was unable to slay the Medusa. In time, the Gods lent him a magical sword, a magical shield and a magical helmet. Using these tools, he slew the Medusa and completed his quest. Unlike most people who play D&D, he returned the magical sword, the magical shield and the magical helmet to their rightful owners.

25. I chose this quote because it is brilliant and it comes from Mae West. There were tens of thousands of quotes to choose from for this chapter. Some were brilliant, but came from obscure sources. Others came from famous sources, but were bland and dull.

26. From **THE RAMBLER**, (#31), written by Samuel Johnson and originally published Tuesday, July 3, 1750.

27. From **MARK TWAIN'S NOTEBOOK**, November 1894. The quote is referenced again in **WHEN IN DOUBT, TELL THE TRUTH**, a speech given by Samuel Clemens on March 8, 1906. There were many other worthy quotes on this topic that were not selected from sources as varied as Will Rogers to Red Skelton.

28. From the album **BIG BAD JOHN** (1962). This was a huge hit for Jimmy Dean and opened the door to a musical career that spanned 40 years, as well as a supporting role in a James Bond movie and the sale of several million breakfast sausages. It's good work if you can get it.

29. This principle is derived from "organic theory" or "system theory." There are many references in literature to the concept of the whole being more than the sum of the parts. Aristotle wrote about it in the fourth century B.C. Adam Smith wrote about it in an

inquiry into the nature and causes of the wealth of Nations (1776). His use of a pin factory as an example is a classic and still frequently used. Karl Marx references this phenomenon in his writings of the mid-1800s. Ludwig Von Bertalanffy developed general system theory in the mid-1900s.

A more contemporary example can be found in Super Bowl XLII. On paper, the Patriots were supposed to win and win big. Yet, the Giants won. The rules were the same for both teams, the salary cap was the same for both teams, and the technology available was the same for both teams. In fact, there was simply no area where one team held an advantage or privilege the other team did not. The Giants simply made their parts add up to more than the Patriots did.

30. From **KING LEAR** (1606). Act I, scene II. This play has been made into a motion picture several times. If you choose to rent one of these, the 1974 version starring James Earl Jones is probably the best choice.

31. From the movie **SATURDAY NIGHT FEVER** (1977).

32. **THE DEFINITIVE BOOK OF BODY LANGUAGE** by Barbara and Allan Pease (Bantam, 2006)

33. From **CATCHER IN THE WRY** (1986, Jove Press). The details are somewhat sketchy, because I read the book 20 years ago. The incident occurred on a flight and involved a rookie infielder and a surly veteran, possibly Richie Allen. The rookie developed airsickness and threw up. When he did so, he caught all of the vomit in his hands. The veteran (Allen?) simply looked over and said "good hands."

34. The hand placement suggested in this exercise is based on standard American table manners. It is appropriate most of time. Business etiquette will occasionally require you to keep your hands in plain view during dinner. In those situations, you should rest your wrists on the edge of the table.

35. **SATURDAY NIGHT LIVE**, Season #2, Episode #14, NBC broadcast, 26 February 1977

36. From **TRILBY** (1894) by George du Maurier. Svengali is the original evil hypnotist. He uses his mind control powers to make others bend to his will and commit evil acts on his behalf.

37. From **THE MAN WITH NO ENDORPHINS AND OTHER REFLECTIONS ON SCIENCE**, Random House (1989).

38. From the 1996 movie **HAPPY GILMORE**, starring Adam Sandler as Happy Gilmore. In this scene, Happy is insulting Bob Barker's wardrobe.

39. From **MONTY PYTHON AND THE HOLY GRAIL (1975)**

40. Yogi Berra is possibly the greatest philosopher of the 20th century.

41. Adams was a newspaper columnist and radio personality during the first half of the 20th century. His columns and radio shows routinely involve information gathering, and this quote is an anecdote regarding that process.

42. From the movie **WEIRD SCIENCE** (1985).

43. From the 1970 soundtrack album **I WALK THE LINE**. The song **FLESH AND BLOOD** was written as a love song to June Carter.

44. From **TERRE DES HOMMES** (1939). Translated into English as **WIND, SAND AND STARS** (1939).

45. From **YOUNG FRANKENSTEIN** (1974), directed by Mel Brooks.

46. From National Lampoon's **ANIMAL HOUSE** (1978).

47. From **THE FINE ART OF FLIRTING** (1986) Fireside Press.

48. Historical references for this quote are sparse, as are references to Anita Wise herself. She played a waitress in one episode of "Seinfeld". This quote is often incorrectly attributed to Rita Rudner.

49. This is the ending tag line from **BATMAN** the TV series, which ran from 1966 to 1968. It has been in syndication ever since. Most readers will be familiar with the television

series. Let me state for the record that Adam West is the greatest Batman of them all.

50. From **STAR TREK: GENERATIONS** (1994).

51. From National Lampoon's **ANIMAL HOUSE** (1978).

52. From **HAMLET** (1603). The line is delivered by Polonius during a long-winded and confusing speech, thus intensifying the irony of the line.

53. Written by Ray Davies and released as a single in 1982. From **COME DANCING WITH THE KINKS: THE BEST OF THE KINKS 1977-1986**.

54. From **THE DEVIL'S DICTIONARY** (1911). This dictionary reinterprets words in the English language with a special emphasis lampooning cant and political doubletalk.

55. From **MONTY PYTHON AND THE HOLY GRAIL** (1975).

56. From **THE WIZARD OF OZ** (1939).

Bibliography

Traditional Publications:

Copeland, D. and Louis, R. (1998). **HOW TO SUCCEED WITH WOMEN**. New York: Reward Books

Kuriansky, J. (2004). **THE COMPLETE IDIOT'S GUIDE TO DATING, (3RD EDITION)**. New York: Alpha Books

Huffman, F. and Wolff, P. (2007). **A PRACTICAL HANDBOOK FOR THE BOYFRIEND, A: FOR EVERY GUY WHO WANTS TO BE ONE/FOR EVERY GIRL WHO WANTS TO BUILD ONE**. New York: Hyperion

E-Book:

DeAngelo, D. (2001). **DOUBLE YOUR DATING: WHAT EVERY MAN SHOULD KNOW ABOUT HOW TO BE MORE SUCCESSFUL WITH WOMEN**. Las Vegas: DDMI

Websites:

http://msn.match.com/cp/msn/article/articleindex.html

http://dating.personals.yahoo.com/singles/datingtips/

http://dating.about.com/

http://www.topdatingtips.com/

http://www.askmen.com/dating/

http://advice.eharmony.com/

www.ingramcontent.com/pod-product-compliance
Lightning Source LLC
LaVergne TN
LVHW020655100826
845148LV00012B/2506